Issues today

Human Rights

Contents

Chapter One: Our Human Rights

Chapter Two: Children's Rights

A resource for KS3

About Key Stage 3

Key Stage 3 refers to the first three years of secondary schooling, normally years 7, 8 and 9, during which pupils are aged between 11 and 14.

This series is also suitable for Scottish P7, S1 and S2 students.

About Issues Today

Issues Today is a series of resource books on contemporary social issues for Key Stage 3 pupils. It is based on the concept behind the popular *Issues* series for 14- to 18-year-olds, also published by Independence.

Each volume contains information from a variety of sources, including government reports and statistics, newspaper and magazine articles, surveys and polls, academic research and literature from charities and lobby groups. The information has been tailored to an 11 to 14 age group; it has been rewritten and presented in a simple, straightforward format to be accessible to Key Stage 3 pupils.

In addition, each *Issues Today* title features handy tasks and assignments based on the information contained in the book, for use in class, for homework or as a revision aid.

Issues Today can be used as a learning resource in a variety of Key Stage 3 subjects, including English, Science, History, Geography, PSHE, Citizenship, Sex and Relationships Education and Religious Education.

About this book

Human Rights is the twenty-fifth volume in the *Issues Today* series. It looks at the basic rights all humans have, the rights of children and how these rights can be abused. There are laws in place to protect our human rights, but despite this many people still have their rights taken away and are subjected to slavery, torture and inhumane treatment. Around the world 126 million children work in hazardous conditions and millions of young people are denied their right to education. What are our human rights and how are they protected?

Human Rights offers a useful overview of the many issues involved in this topic. However, at the end of each article is a URL for the relevant organisation's website, which can be visited by pupils who want to carry out further research.

Because the information in this book is gathered from a number of different sources, pupils should think about the origin of the text and critically evaluate the information that is presented. Does the source have a particular bias or agenda? Are you being presented with facts or opinions? Do you agree with the writer?

At the end of each chapter there are two pages of activities relating to the articles and issues raised in that chapter. The 'Brainstorm' questions can be done as a group or individually after reading the articles. This should prompt some ideas and lead on to further activities. Some suggestions for such activities are given under the headings 'Oral', 'Moral Dilemmas', 'Research', 'Written' and 'Design' that follow the 'Brainstorm' questions.

For more information about *Issues Today* and its sister series, *Issues* (for pupils aged 14 to 18), please visit the Independence website.

www.independence.co.uk

A resource for KS3

Human Rights

Editor: **Claire Owen**

ISSUE
25

Independence
Educational Publishers
Cambridge

First published by Independence

The Studio, High Green, Great Shelford

Cambridge CB22 5EG

England

© Independence 2009

British Library Cataloguing in Publication Data

Human rights – (Issues Today; v. 25)

1. Human Rights

I. Series II. Owen, Claire

323-dc22

ISBN-13: 978 1 86168 496 7

Acknowledgements

The publisher is grateful for permission to reproduce the following material.

While every care has been taken to trace and acknowledge copyright, the publisher tenders its apology for any accidental infringement or where copyright has proved untraceable. The publisher would be pleased to come to a suitable arrangement in any such case with the rightful owner.

Chapter One: Our Human Rights

Introducing human rights, © British Institute of Human Rights, *What are our human rights?,* © Amnesty International UK, *Human rights timeline,* © British Institute of Human Rights, *What human rights mean to me,* © Amnesty International UK, *Modern-day slavery,* © My Learning / York Museums Trust, *Modern slavery map,* © Free the Slaves, *Torture: myths and facts,* © Medical Foundation for the Care of Victims of Torture, *Inside the Human Rights Act,* © Liberty.

Chapter Two: Children's Rights

Children's rights: the facts, © Children's Rights Alliance for England, *Children's rights,* © UNICEF, *Child labour,* © Save the Children, *Your rights,* © UNICEF, *All equal?,* © Children's Rights Alliance for England, *Smacking,* © Children are Unbeatable! Alliance, *Smacking is a decision for parents,* © Telegraph Group Limited.

All illustrations, including the cover, are by Don Hatcher.

Printed in Great Britain by MWL Print Group Ltd.

Claire Owen

Cambridge

May, 2009

Introducing human rights

What are human rights?

Human rights belong to everyone. They are the basic rights we all have simply because we are human, regardless of who we are, where we live or what we do. Human rights allow us to do well, to reach our potential and take part fully in society. Human rights cover many parts of everyday life, from the rights to food, shelter, education and health to freedoms of thought, religion and expression.

Human rights are underpinned by core values or principles, including fairness, respect, equality, dignity, autonomy, universality and participation. Human rights issues, values and principles are expressed through internationally-agreed laws. These laws exist as a way to make core human rights values real in people's lives.

> 66 Human rights are not a privilege conferred by government. They are every human being's entitlement by virtue of his humanity. 99
>
> **Mother Teresa**

Where do human rights come from?

The ideas behind human rights have been present throughout history in many different societies and civilizations. However, the modern concept of human rights came about in the twentieth century as a response to the events of the Second World War, particularly the crimes committed during the Holocaust. States came together in 1948 at the United Nations to agree the Universal Declaration of Human Rights (UDHR) – the most famous and probably most important human rights document.

The fundamental rights and freedoms outlined in the UDHR are expressed in international human rights agreements that are legally binding on states that agree to them.

In total there are nine core UN human rights treaties:

► The International Covenant on Civil and Political Rights (ICCPR);

► The International Covenant on Economic, Social and Cultural Rights (ICESCR);

► The Convention Against Torture (CAT);

► The Convention on the Elimination of Discrimination Against Women (CEDAW);

► The Convention on the Elimination of Racial Discrimination (CERD);

► The Convention on the Rights of the Child (CRC);

► The International Convention on the Protection of the Rights of all Migrant Workers and Members of their Families (the UK has not signed this Convention);

► The International Convention for the Protection of all Persons from Enforced Disappearances (not yet in force; the UK has not signed this Convention);

► The Convention on the Rights of Persons with Disabilities (CRPD) (the UK has signed, but not yet ratified, this Convention).

Introducing human rights

Countries have also come together to agree regional human rights treaties such as the European Convention on Human Rights, the American Convention on Human Rights and the African Charter on Human and People's Rights. These treaties contain some, but not all, of the rights expressed in the UDHR. Many countries also have their own human rights laws – in the UK we have the Human Rights Act.

What kinds of rights are protected by human rights laws?

There are many human rights, which reflect different areas of our lives covering civil, political, economic, social, cultural and environmental aspects. All human rights are linked – limiting one right has a negative effect on other rights, while taking steps to fulfil a right allows the enjoyment of other rights. For example, restricting the right to health by not providing an adequate healthcare system may impact on other rights in a negative way such as the right to life. Improving the right to education through an effective education system for all can support the enjoyment of other rights such as the right to work.

Different human rights laws focus on different rights. Some international treaties focus on particular rights, such as the Convention against Torture. Other international treaties protect the rights of certain groups, for example women, children and disabled people. The existence of these treaties does not give these groups any additional rights, but recognises the particular discrimination and difficulties some groups face in claiming their human rights.

DID YOU KNOW

The UK has signed all of the core international human rights treaties, except for the Migrant Worker's Convention and the International Convention for the Protection of all Persons from Enforced Disappearances.

Can human rights ever be taken away or limited?

No one can have their human rights completely taken away – even if they have not met their responsibilities or have compromised the rights of others. Some human rights are absolute, which means they can never be limited or restricted, in any circumstances – for example the right not to be tortured or treated in an inhuman or degrading way. However, most human rights are not absolute and can be limited or restricted in certain circumstances. For example, if someone writes hate speech encouraging murder against an ethnic group, their freedom of expression may be limited to protect the safety of others. Social services may decide to remove a child from their home and place them in care if they have evidence that they are being abused by their parents, thus restricting the right to respect for family life.

> 66 Human rights are inscribed in the hearts of the people; they were there long before lawmakers drafted their first proclamation. 99
>
> **Mary Robinson, Former United Nations High Commissioner for Human Rights**

If human rights cannot be taken away, then how come there are so many human rights abuses happening in the world?

The fact that we all have human rights does not mean that they are always respected. It is clear that human rights abuses and violations continue to take place in different parts of the world, including in the UK. In order to make human rights a reality in all people's lives, it is essential that people know what their rights are and know how to claim them. It is equally important that those responsible for protecting and respecting people's rights are aware of their obligations and are held to account for human rights abuses.

Introducing human rights

Do individuals hold responsibilities to each other?

Human rights recognise that we all live alongside each other, and everyone else has rights too. This is why most rights are non-absolute and can be limited or restricted in certain circumstances. If we compromise others' human rights, we are subject to laws that may limit our own rights as a result. For example, if we commit a crime we may be sent to jail, thus restricting our right to liberty. But more than this, human rights can be viewed as part of the relationships we have to each other and society as a whole, and therefore we have an ethical responsibility to respect each other's rights – even when in some instances those rights conflict with one's own. The state is ultimately accountable for balancing these sometimes conflicting rights.

Which human rights laws apply in the UK?

The main source of human rights law in the UK is the Human Rights Act, which came into force in 2000. The Human Rights Act includes most of the rights that are contained in the European Convention on Human Rights into UK law. The UK signed up to the European Convention in 1951.

> 66 Where, after all, do universal human rights begin? In small places, close to home. 99
>
> **Eleanor Roosevelt**

Why are human rights relevant to the UK?

Human rights belong to everyone in the UK and are relevant to many of the situations people experience and the decisions people make on a daily basis. The Human Rights Act provides an important safety net for protecting us all, particularly when we are facing disadvantage or discrimination, or are at our most vulnerable. The Human Rights Act also provides a useful framework for public authorities – including central and local government departments, hospitals, state schools and social services departments – within which decisions can be made and different rights and interests can be balanced.

However, in the UK we usually only hear about human rights being used by those who may have compromised other people's rights, such as criminals and terrorists. Although these groups still keep their core human rights, many of their rights will be restricted. But we rarely hear about how the Human Rights Act has been used, for example, to protect older people who are being abused in care homes, to make sure that disabled children are provided with transport to get to school and to protect women from domestic violence. There are many other examples of how the Human Rights Act has been used to improve the lives of people in the UK, both in and outside of the courtroom.

Mini glossary

ratified – when a treaty has been formally approved

underpinned – supported by

Holocaust – the systematic killing of millions of Jews by the Nazis during World War II

covenant – a signed agreement

elimination – getting rid of something

fulfil – put into effect or achieve

adequate – good enough

compromised – undermined

violations – acts that ignore rights

ethical – morally right

The above information is reprinted with kind permission from the British Institute of Human Rights. © British Institute of Human Rights

www.bihr.org.uk

What are our human rights?

WE ARE ALL BORN FREE AND EQUAL. Human rights are what every human being needs to live a healthy and fulfilled life and to take part fully in society. They are entitlements – you have them just because you are human. The Universal Declaration of Human Rights (UDHR) was drawn up by the United Nations and presented to the world on 10 December 1948.

Human rights are:

▶ **universal** – they apply to everyone equally;

▶ **inalienable** – they cannot be taken away from people;

▶ **indivisible** – they are all connected: failure to protect one right can lead to abuse of other rights, just as taking action to fulfil one right can lead to the fulfilment of other rights.

The Universal Declaration of Human Rights

Article 1 – We are all born free. We all have our own thoughts and ideas. We should all be treated in the same way.

Article 2 – These rights belong to everybody; whether we are rich or poor, whatever country we live in, whatever sex or whatever colour we are, whatever language we speak, whatever we think or whatever we believe.

Article 3 – We all have the right to life, and to live in freedom and safety.

Article 4 – Nobody has any right to make us a slave. We cannot make anyone else our slave.

Article 5 – Nobody has any right to hurt us or to torture us.

Article 6 – We all have the same right to use the law.

Article 7 – The law is the same for everyone. It must treat us all fairly.

Article 8 – We can all ask for the law to help us when we are not treated fairly.

Article 9 – Nobody has the right to put us in prison without a good reason, to keep us there or to send us away from our country.

Article 10 – If someone is accused of breaking the law they have the right to a fair and public trial.

Article 11 – Nobody should be blamed for doing something until it has been proved that they did it. If people say we did something bad, we have the right to show this was not true. Nobody should punish us for something that we did not do, or for doing something which was not against the law when we did it.

Article 12 – Nobody should try to harm our good name. Nobody has the right to come into our home, open our letters, or bother us or our family without a very good reason.

Article 13 – We all have the right to go where we want to in our own country and to travel abroad as we wish.

What are our human rights?

Article 14 – If we are frightened of being badly treated in our own country, we all have the right to escape to another country to be safe.

Article 15 – We all have the right to belong to a country.

Article 16 – Every adult has the right to marry and have a family if they want to. Men and women have the same rights when they are married and when they are separated.

Article 17 – Everyone has the right to own things or share them. Nobody should take our things from us without a good reason.

Article 18 – We all have the right to believe in what we want to believe, to have a religion, or to change it if we want.

Article 19 – We all have the right to make up our own minds, to think what we like, to say what we think, and to share our ideas with other people wherever they live, through books, radio, television and in other ways.

Article 20 – We all have the right to meet our friends and to work together in peace to defend our rights. Nobody can make us join a group if we don't want to.

Article 21 – We all have the right to take part in the government of our country. Every adult should be allowed to choose their own leaders from time to time and should have a vote which should be made in secret.

Article 22 – We all have the right to a home, to have enough money to live on and medical help if we are ill. We should all be allowed to enjoy music, art, craft, sport and to make use of our skills.

Article 23 – Every adult has the right to a job, to get a fair wage for their work, and to join a trade union.

Article 24 – We all have the right to rest from work and relax.

Article 25 – We all have the right to a good life, with enough food, clothing, housing, and healthcare. Mothers and children, people without work, old and disabled people all have the right to help.

Article 26 – We all have the right to an education, and to finish primary school, which should be free. We should be able to learn a career, or to make use of all our skills. We should learn about the United Nations and about how to get on with other people and respect their rights. Our parents have the right to choose how and what we will learn.

Article 27 – We all have the right to our own way of life, and to enjoy the good things that science and learning bring.

Article 28 – We have a right to peace and order so we can all enjoy rights and freedoms in our own country and all over the world.

Article 29 – We have a duty to other people, and we should protect their rights and freedoms.

Article 30 – Nobody can take these rights and freedoms away from us.

www.amnesty.org.uk

This simplified version of the Universal Declaration of Human Rights is by Amnesty International UK. © Amnesty International UK

Human rights timeline

THE MODERN CONCEPT OF HUMAN RIGHTS has its foundations in the Universal Declaration of Human Rights, adopted by the United Nations in the aftermath of the Second World War. However, the ideas behind human rights have been present throughout history in many different societies and civilizations. This timeline explores some of the roots and origins of human rights and how they have developed throughout history into the conception we have today.

1760BC — In Babylon King Hammurabi draws up the 'Code of Hammurabi', an early legal document that promises to 'make justice reign in the kingdom ... and promote the good of the people.'

In India, Buddha preaches morality, reverence for life, non-violence and right conduct. — **c528BC – 486BC**

c26-33AC — In Palestine, Jesus Christ preaches morality, tolerance, justice, forgiveness and love.

In Saudi Arabia, Prophet Mohammed teaches the principles of equality, justice and compassion revealed in The Qur'an. — **613-632**

1215 — In England the Magna Carta is agreed, limiting the power of the King and giving free men the right to be judged by their peers.

The English Parliament agrees the English Bill of Rights, reducing the power of the monarch and including the right to be free from torture and to punishment without trial. — **1689**

1789 — In France, the National Assembly agrees the French Declaration of the Rights of Man and of the Citizen, which guarantees the rights to liberty, equality, property, security and resistance to oppression.

The United States Congress agrees the US Bill of Rights, amending the US Constitution to include rights to trial by jury, freedom of expression, speech, belief and assembly. — **1791**

1833 — The British Parliament abolishes slavery in the British Empire through the Slavery Abolition Act.

The International Labour Organisation (ILO) is established to advocate for rights in labour law, e.g. employment discrimination and forced labour. — **1919**

Human rights timeline

The National Council for Civil Liberties (usually known as 'Liberty') is established, a non-governmental organisation that seeks to protect civil liberties and promote human rights for everyone in England And Wales.

1934

1945

The United Nations (UN) is created 'to reaffirm faith in human rights, in the dignity and worth of the human person ....'

The Universal Declaration of Human Rights is adopted by the UN.

1948

1950

The European Convention on Human Rights is adopted by the Council of Europe. The UK signed up to the Convention in 1951.

Amnesty International is created by British lawyer Peter Benenson.

1961

1968

The first world conference on human rights is held in Tehran.

The Convention on the Rights of the Child is adopted and opened for signature by the UN, entering into force in 1990. This is the most widely-ratified human rights treaty; only the USA and Somalia have not ratified the CRC.

1989

1998

The Human Rights Act 1998 is adopted by the UK Parliament, making most of the rights contained in the European Convention on Human Rights part of UK law. The Act entered into force on 2 October 2000.

The Northern Ireland Human Rights Commission is set up to promote awareness of the importance of human rights in Northern Ireland.

1999

2007

The Equality and Human Rights Commission is launched in Great Britain. The Commission works to end discrimination, reduce inequality, promote human rights and build good relations.

Mini glossary

aftermath – the period following an event

reign – rule over all; have power or influence

preach – to urge or speak in favour of something

reverence – respect

The Qur'an – the main religious text of Islam

peers – group of equals

advocate – support and defend

www.bihr.org.uk

What human rights mean to me

> My life today is complex. It is a life in three parts, everything is either my life before the war, my life during the war, or my life after the war. All three aspects, including the negative parts, have shaped me and my views, they make me what I am whether I like it or not.
>
> I have come to know what it means to have peace in your life, because I have experienced the lack of it and what that does to your spirit. And I have come to understand that when people disregard or lose respect for their own life they are damaging something that is sacrosanct.
>
> Before the war I just remember the peace, the day-to-day life of going to school, and on the way back playing football and swimming. Simple. I don't think I had any idea how privileged and special that was until it was no longer happening. For me, from a very early age, there was an appreciation for life itself all around me. There was a care from all of our community, not just from my immediate family. All that changed so quickly and suddenly, and horribly, but the early years grounded me and really helped me later.
>
> Human rights are about recognising human dignity and the right to life. When people are unwilling to pay attention if others are abused, killed, this brings out the worst in everyone and eventually affects the type of society. For me, human rights are very real, because I have seen the suffering that happens when they are disregarded. People who live in comfort often take a lot for granted. Not everyone can wake up in the morning and turn the tap on and see water pour out. And just the privilege of being able to dream, and being able to achieve that dream. I have seen people lose the strength to even dream, I have seen people who feel completely hopeless.
>
> My own hope is that I can help make people around the world aware of other people's situations, so that no-one turns a blind eye when terrible things happen. I hope to have people who care, a generation with more of a world view, who think beyond their own environment. Our common humanity and human rights are more important than our nationality or socio-econ status. Once we all know that, it will ground how we treat each other, respect each other. "

Ishmael Beah,

Former child soldier and author of *A Long Way Gone.*

DID YOU KNOW ? *Amnesty International documented cases of torture and other cruel, inhuman or degrading treatment in more than 81 countries in 2007.*

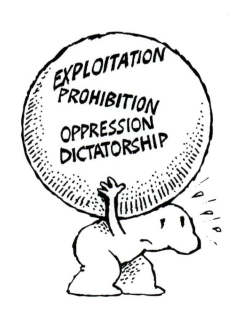

What human rights mean to me

If you are lucky enough to live in a reasonably well-ordered society, it is easy to take human rights rather for granted. But as soon as things start to get rougher they quickly become more and more important. And when the situation really falls apart, the fundamental human rights are all that matter.

I am thinking, for example, of what I saw in Afghanistan under the Taliban. The small number of Afghan women who had managed to carve out a limited amount of freedom saw even that swept away. The Taliban were banning education for girls and largely confining the female half of the population to the home. At the same time they were prohibiting music, and television and much else. The Taliban were in many ways, of course, an utter disaster in human rights terms. But it has to be said that in those early days significant numbers of Afghans welcomed them in Kabul and the south and the east. And this was in part because the Taliban had imposed a rough kind of order that meant people felt a little safer. In the previous years the country had fallen apart so badly that many Afghans craved above all else those fundamental human rights – the right to life and a degree of security.

Last year I was kidnapped in Gaza and held captive for nearly four months by a group called the Army of Islam.

During that time I did not have the freedom to choose anything. What I ate, what I drank, and whether I lived or died – all of that was decided by my captors. For me personally, things had very much fallen apart, and in the starkest terms I was forced to appreciate fully the meaning of the most basic human rights.

But long before I was forced into that cell in Gaza, my view of the world had been shaped in important ways by those who had done most to expand the boundaries of freedom. There was Gandhi marching to the sea – on his way to make salt in defiance of unjust colonial laws. There was Mandela passing a quarter of a century in his cell before emerging to bring down the Apartheid system that I had seen as a child. And in Alabama there was Rosa Parks saying 'no', she should not have to give up her seat on the bus for a white man.

If you want to believe and argue that mankind is advancing – if only very gradually – towards something better, then surely the best evidence of that is the rising, worldwide awareness of the notion of human rights. We have a long way to go, but the universal declaration of those rights helps shine a light on the path ahead.

Alan Johnston, BBC correspondent

BBC correspondent Alan Johnston's book *Kidnapped* is a selection of his best journalism from Gaza and Afghanistan, a moving account of his 114 days in captivity, and his reflections on survival, solidarity and freedom.

www.amnesty.org.uk

The Ishmael Beah and Alan Johnston interviews are reproduced with kind permission from Amnesty Magazine. © Amnesty International UK

Mini glossary

sacrosanct – *sacred; too important to be taken away or interfered with*

privilege – *an advantage not everybody has*

socio-econ status – *socioeconomic status; a person's position in society based on their social class and earnings*

priority – *the most important thing*

Taliban – *Islamic fundamentalist group in control in Afghanistan*

prohibiting – *banning*

colonial laws – *laws made by settlers who have taken control of another country*

Apartheid system – *policy of racial separation that took place in South Africa and discriminated against black South Africans*

Modern-day slavery

WHEN YOU HEAR THE WORD 'SLAVERY' what do you think of? Do you think of slaves in the past being transported across the Atlantic in appalling conditions and forced to work on plantations in the West Indies? Or do you think of slaves being transported across many different seas and land borders today and who are being forced to work in terrible conditions all over the world, right now?

The abolition of the Trans-Atlantic Slave Trade in 1807 marked the beginning of the end of the slave trade (slavery in the colonies was abolished in 1833). The numbers involved had been huge – over 12 million African men, women and children were forced into slavery. Yet today there are over twice that many people in enforced slavery!

It is estimated that there are some 27 million slaves across the globe today. Although slavery has not affected one single continent to the same degree since the abolition, as unimaginable as it seems, slavery still continues in the 21st century.

What is a modern day 'slave'?

Slavery today takes many different forms. A 'slave' today is defined by Anti-Slavery International as being someone who is:

▶ Forced to work – through mental or physical threat.

▶ Owned or controlled by an 'employer', usually through mental or physical abuse or threatened abuse.

▶ Dehumanised, treated as a commodity or bought and sold as 'property'.

▶ Physically constrained or has restrictions placed on his or her freedom of movement.

Slaves are under the complete control of another person and are often treated violently. They get very little pay for the work they do (or none at all) and get barely enough food and shelter to keep them alive. In fact, the lives of slaves today are not very different from those of slaves 200 hundred years ago.

This is in spite of the fact that slavery is banned in most of the countries where it is practised, and that one of the 'articles' in the UN Universal Declaration of Human Rights states:

❝ *No one shall be held in slavery or servitude; slavery and the slave trade shall be prohibited in all their forms.* ❞

Article 4, Universal Declaration of Human Rights

Types of slavery today

Bonded labour

This is where a person is forced to work in order to pay a debt, which simply keeps on growing (they can never pay it off). People often become bonded labourers after being tricked into taking a loan. Sometimes this loan can be for as little as the cost of medicine for a sick child. To repay the debt, many are forced to work long hours – sometimes seven days a week, 365 days a year.

Forced labour

This is when a person is forced to work under threats of violence, homelessness and starvation etc. Forced labour especially affects people who are illegally recruited by individuals, governments or political parties and forced to work.

Slavery by descent

If someone is a slave 'by descent' this means that they have been born into slavery. They may have been born into an economic class or ethnic group that is viewed by others as being exploitable.

Sex slavery

Sex slavery is when a person is forced into prostitution. Women and children are often the victim of people traffickers who kidnap, buy or lure them with promises of good jobs and then put them to work as prostitutes. Thousands of women have been brought into Western Europe from poorer Eastern European countries to work in brothels or on the streets.

www.mylearning.org

Modern slavery map

North America

Slaves in the US come from 60 countries and have been found in 90 cities. They are enslaved in cleaning houses, working on farms and forced into the sex industry. Trafficking involves deception and ongoing exploitation – both marks of slavery. An estimated 50% of slavery in the United States is in the commercial sex industry and the other 50% is in agriculture, domestic service, manufacturing and other industries.

14,500+: Estimated number of slaves trafficked into the US annually.

Europe and Eurasia

Traffickers often target young women in Russia and Eastern Europe for forced prostitution in Western Europe, Israel, the Gulf States and Japan. Others caught in slavery – trafficked from other regions like Africa, as well as trafficked internally – are forced to work in agriculture, food processing and the service sector – often after being lied to by recruiting agents.

Hundreds of thousands: People estimated to be trafficked into slavery in Europe and Eurasia.

Latin America and Caribbean

Many people in Latin America and the Caribbean are vulnerable to slavery at home and being trafficked abroad. The domestic enslavement of children has been illegal in Haiti for longer than any other country, yet the practice continues, affecting as many as one in ten children. Hundreds of thousands are held in Brazil. The fruits of their labour are exported around the world. The Brazilian government has stepped up enforcement of their own law. The result? 6,000-7,000 freed from slavery each year.

1,320,000: Estimated number of people enslaved in Latin America and the Caribbean.

Africa and Middle East

Africa suffers from a high level of internal and external slavery. Brokers buy and traffic children within and between West African countries. Slaves work in cocoa, coffee, cotton, fishery, mines or as domestic servants or prostitutes. They may also be trafficked on to Europe, the Middle East and Japan, forced to fight by paramilitary forces (as with child soldiers in Uganda) or suffer from state-sanctioned slavery (Sudan). Several Gulf States are destination points for slaves trafficked from Asia and Africa.

920,000: Estimated number of people enslaved in Africa and the Middle East.

Asia and Pacific

The largest number of slaves in the world live in Pakistan, India and Nepal, where as many as 18 million workers are held as slaves – working for generations to repay small loans. The Chinese and Burmese governments participate in slavery. Indonesian fisheries buy or abduct children and sell the product in the West. Malaysia and the Philippines suffer internal enslavement in domestic service and trafficking into sexual exploitation in Gulf States and Japan. Japan, the top user of slave labour among rich countries, is a destination point for 40-50,000 women trafficked annually into the sex industry.

24 million: Estimated number of people enslaved in Asia.

www.freetheslaves.net

The above information is reprinted with kind permission from Free the Slaves.
© Free the Slaves

Torture: myths and facts

TORTURE WAS ONCE A PRACTICE that provoked universal condemnation. States that used torture to repress their citizens were called to account by the international community. Yet in recent years some have sought to justify the use of torture as a means to the end of keeping the public safe from harm.

Much of the debate has been prompted by the global threat of terrorism, which is undoubtedly a serious and pressing issue. By pitching national security against the use of torture, some governments and leading thinkers have sought to dress up torture as 'interrogation', or to legitimise its use.

The current misleading and inaccurate information surrounding the issue of torture has given rise to a new mythology. Here we seek to destroy some of those myths and describe the reality of torture that we see through the experience of our clients from countries around the world.

MYTH: Torture works

FACT: Torture is categorically ineffective in extracting information. In the experience of thousands of survivors seen by the MF, most people subjected to extreme levels of psychological and physical pain and suffering will say anything and even sign false confessions to make the torture stop. Any information which may be extracted under torture is therefore unreliable.

Information extracted under torture is also inadmissible in a court of law. Under Article 15 of the UN Convention against Torture and Other Cruel, Inhuman or Degrading Treatment or Punishment, 'any statement which is established to have been made as a result of torture shall not be invoked as evidence in any proceedings, except against a person accused of torture as evidence that the statement was made'.

www.torturecare.org.uk

The information on these pages is reprinted with kind permission from the Medical Foundation for the Care of Victims of Torture. © Medical Foundation for the Care of Victims of Torture

MYTH: Torture is a means to an end

FACT: The 'ticking time bomb' argument is that if by torturing a person a catastrophe could be avoided, then torturing that person would be an acceptable means of saving the lives of thousands of others. The human rights of one person are pitched against the safety of thousands in an emotionally persuasive argument that has gathered much support in the wake of 9/11 and the climate of fear of war and terrorism.

However, the situation is a hypothetical extreme with no basis in reality. It also assumes that torture would be limited to one particular incident and that the information sought would actually be given under torture. Yet, as history shows, to allow any abhorrent practice once is to set a dangerous precedent.

Torture not only degrades the victim, it degrades the torturer and the society that allows it.

MYTH: Only criminals and terrorists are tortured

FACT: In 2007, the MF received requests for help from some 2,000 people who had fled 95 countries across the world.

The majority of MF clients report having been targeted due to their race, ethnic origin, gender, religious, cultural or political beliefs. Political activists and journalists are often targeted by the authorities for voicing their opposition to government policies. Many others find themselves falsely connected to terrorist incidents with which they had no involvement. Many people are targeted for torture during conflicts, where torture is used to create a climate of fear and to force people to flee.

The husbands, wives and children of people targeted are frequently targeted simply by association in an effort to get to someone else.

Torture: myths and facts

MYTH: Torture only has lasting effects for the victim

FACT: The torturer's goal is to repress and dehumanise the victim. While the act of torture is directed at an individual, the effects are widespread, affecting those who are witnesses, others who may hear the torture taking place and the families and communities of torture survivors. Torture has an effect on the lives of any of those who it touches – including those who commit torture.

The effects of torture can last a lifetime. In addition to post traumatic stress disorder, depression, anxiety, flashbacks, nightmares and insomnia, torture survivors can end up avoiding interacting with other people and distancing themselves from the outside world.

More broadly, the consequences for societies where torture is permitted are severe. Where torture is tolerated as a seemingly useful and acceptable technique to keep communities safe or to repress others sets a dangerous precedent that human rights are expendable.

MYTH: Agents of the UK do not engage in torture

FACT: In March 2008, the Ministry of Defence (MoD) admitted breaching the European Convention on Human Rights in relation to the death of an Iraqi civilian and the torture of nine others in September 2003. In July 2008, the MoD paid the families almost £3 million in compensation for the murder of Baha Mousa and the torture and abuse of nine others.

The family of Iraqi receptionist Mr Mousa brought the action against the MoD following his death and a coroner's report which identified 93 separate injuries to his body.

A hearing found that troops had ignored the 1972 ruling by the UK government which banned the use of hooding, stress positions and deprivation of food, noise and sleep. One soldier pleaded guilty to inhumane treatment and six others, including the commanding officer, were acquitted of negligence and abuse. No one was convicted of killing Mr. Mousa.

Public opinion on human rights

The Human Rights Convention requires suspects to be treated the same, regardless of whether they have British or foreign nationality. Do you support the following proposal?

Britain should have, and use, the right to deport foreigners suspected by the intelligence services, even if there is not enough courtroom evidence to bring them to trial, and they might be sent to countries where they could be tortured.

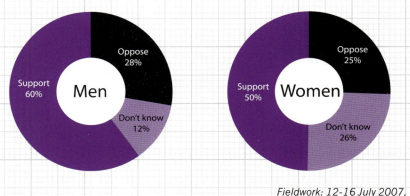

Men: Oppose 28%, Support 60%, Don't know 12%

Women: Oppose 25%, Support 50%, Don't know 26%

Fieldwork: 12-16 July 2007.
Source: YouGov, on behalf of Migration Watch (www.yougov.com)

Mini glossary

condemnation – strong disapproval

abhorrent – hateful or offensive

repress – control

interrogation – questioning

extract – to draw out, often using force

hypothetical – based on assumptions, not facts

precedent – an example that is used to justify similar occurrences at a later time

expendable – something that can be sacrificed

post traumatic stress disorder – an anxiety disorder caused by a traumatic experience

Inside the Human Rights Act

What is the Human Rights Act?

The Human Rights Act is a written law passed in 1998 which is in force in England and Wales. The human rights that are contained within this law are based on the articles of the European Convention on Human Rights. That is why, when we talk about the rights granted by the Human Rights Act we often refer to them as 'Convention rights'.

Who can use it?

The Human Rights Act may be used by every person resident in England or Wales regardless of whether or not they are a British citizen or a foreign national, a child or an adult, a prisoner or a member of the public.

What does it actually do?

The Act 'gives further effect' to rights and freedoms guaranteed under the European Convention on Human Rights. What this actually means is that it does two things:

▶ Judges must read and give effect to legislation (other laws) in a way which is compatible with the Convention rights.

▶ It is unlawful for a public authority to act in a way which is incompatible with a Convention right.

What does that mean for me?

Well, if you can show that a public authority has interfered with any of the rights recognised by the Convention you can take action in a number of different ways. For example:

▶ You could write to the public authority concerned and remind them of their legal obligations under the Human Rights Act and ask them to correct the situation.

▶ If you went to court the court may find that a particular action (or inaction) of a public authority is (or would be) unlawful. It can tell the public authority to stop interfering with your right or to take action to protect your right.

▶ If the court is satisfied that a provision of a law is incompatible with a Convention right, it may make a formal legal statement that the particular law interferes with human rights.

www.liberty-human-rights.org.uk

What rights does it protect?

▶ The right to life – protects your life, by law. The state is required to investigate suspicious deaths and deaths in custody.

▶ The banning of torture and inhuman treatment – you should never be tortured or treated in an inhuman or degrading way.

▶ Protection against slavery and forced labour – you should not be treated like a slave or subjected to forced labour.

▶ The right to liberty and freedom – you have the right to be free and the state can only imprison you with very good reason – for example, if you are convicted of a crime.

▶ The right to a fair trial and no punishment without law – you are innocent until proven guilty. If accused of a crime, you have the right to hear the evidence against you, in a court of law.

▶ Respect for privacy and family life and the right to marry – protects against unnecessary surveillance or intrusion into your life. You have the right to marry and raise a family.

▶ Freedom of thought, religion and belief – you can believe what you like and practise your religion or beliefs.

▶ Free speech and peaceful protest – you have a right to speak freely and join with others peacefully, to express your views.

▶ No discrimination – everyone's rights are equal. You should not be treated unfairly – because, for example, of your gender, race, sexuality, religion or age.

▶ Protection of property, the right to an education and the right to free elections – protects against state interference with your possessions; means that no child can be denied an education and that elections must be free and fair.

Mini glossary

compatible – *in keeping with; able to exist together*

surveillance – *close observation*

Activities

Brainstorm

Brainstorm to find out what you know about human rights.

1. What are human rights?

    ....

    ....

    ....

2. What is the Universal Declaration of Human Rights?

    ....

    ....

3. What is the Human Rights Act?

    ....

    ....

Oral activities

4. In a group, come up with a list of the human rights you think everyone should have. How are these rights protected in everyday life?

    NOTES...

    ....

    ....

5. Read the article *Modern-day slavery* on page 10. Give a talk outlining the conditions a person living in slavery may have to endure and explaining the types of modern slavery that exist today.

    NOTES...

    ....

Moral Dilemmas

6. Imagine you are a politician voting on whether the UK should be able to deport foreign suspects to countries where they might be tortured. How would you vote and why?

7. Do you think there are any circumstances under which a person should be denied their human rights? Should terrorists and criminals still be entitled to human rights?

Activities

Research activities

8. Do some research into an organisation that protects human rights, such as Amnesty International or Liberty. Visit their website and investigate what their main aims are and what action they take to achieve these aims.

    NOTES..

    ....

    ....

    ....

9. Look at a selection of newspapers and find a news story in which you think somebody has been denied their human rights. Use articles from the United Declaration of Human Rights and the Human Rights Act to outline the ways in which their rights have been abused.

    CONCLUSION...

    ....

    ....

    ....

    ....

Written activities

Complete the following activities in your exercise books or on a sheet of paper.

10. Look at the rights listed in the Universal Declaration of Human Rights. Create a two-column table, with one column for absolute rights and one column for rights which can be limited or restricted. Decide which human rights you think belong in each column.

11. Read about the United Declaration of Human Rights in *What are our rights?* on pages 4-5. Write your own declaration, listing the rights you think everyone should enjoy in your school or community.

Design activities

12. Choose one of the articles from the Universal Declaration of Human Rights and create a poster to illustrate it.

Children's rights: the facts

Children and young people around the world

- There are over four billion children and young people in the world.

- Babies born in the richest countries are expected to live until they are about 79 years old; in the poorest countries life expectancy is just 53 years.

- Estonia in Northern Europe has the smallest child population in the world, at less than half a million. China and India have the biggest populations of children and young people, at close to 345 million each.

- England has over 11 million children and young people – about one in five of the population!

- There are 3.9 million children and young people in the UK living in poverty.

- Norway was the first country to appoint an independent Children's Ombudsperson (in 1981) – a powerful person separate from government who can push for the rights of children and young people.

Young people and the vote

- ▶ Young people can vote from the age of 16 years in Brazil, Cuba, Nicaragua and the Isle of Man.

- ▶ Iran did have the lowest voting age, at 15, but it raised this to 18 in 2007.

- ▶ There are moves in Austria to lower the voting age to 16.

- ▶ In England, the voting age was last reduced in 1967, from 21 to 18.

DID YOU KNOW? *The first country that agreed to follow the Convention on the Rights of the Child was Ghana in Africa in February 1990. The UK agreed to follow it in December 1991.*

Young people and punishment

- In 1669, children and young people petitioned Parliament to ask for an end to harsh and brutal treatment from teachers. Yet it wasn't until 1986 that a law was passed to stop teachers from using any kind of corporal punishment. The proposal was won in Parliament by just one vote!

- Over 9,000 children and young people were permanently excluded from school in 2004/05.

- For every 100,000 children and young people in the UK, 23 are locked up. This is nearly four times the number of children and young people locked up in France and over 100 times the number of children locked up in Finland!

- 18 countries have changed the law to stop parents hitting their children (the date in brackets is when the law was changed) – Sweden (1979), Finland (1983), Norway (1987), Austria (1989), Cyprus (1994), Denmark (1997), Latvia (1998), Croatia (1999), Germany (2000), Bulgaria (2000), Israel (2000), Iceland (2003), Romania (2004), Ukraine (2004), Hungary (2005), Greece (2006), the Netherlands (2007) and New Zealand (2007).

www.getreadyforchange.org.uk

Children's rights

EVERY CHILD AND YOUNG PERSON under 18 has rights and responsibilities. They're protected by the United Nations Convention on the Rights of the Child. It's been signed by every country in the world, except the USA and Somalia. The Convention spells out your rights in a series of 'articles'.

ARTICLE 1 Everyone under the age of 18 has all the rights in this Convention.

ARTICLE 2 The Convention applies to everyone whatever their race, religion, abilities, whatever they think or say, no matter what type of family they come from.

ARTICLE 3 All organisations concerned with children should work towards what is best for you.

ARTICLE 4 Governments should make these rights available to you.

ARTICLE 5 Governments should respect the rights and responsibilities of families to direct and guide their children so that they learn to use their rights properly.

ARTICLE 6 You have the right to life. Governments should ensure that children survive and develop healthily.

ARTICLE 7 You have the right to a legally registered name and nationality. You also have the right to know and, as far as possible, to be cared for by your parents.

ARTICLE 8 Governments should respect children's right to a name, a nationality and family ties.

ARTICLE 9 You should not be separated from your parents unless it is for your own good – for example, if a parent is mistreating or neglecting you. If your parents have separated, you have the right to stay in contact with both parents, unless this might harm you.

ARTICLE 10 Families who live in different countries should be allowed to move between those countries so that parents and children can stay in contact or get back together as a family.

ARTICLE 11 Governments should take steps to stop children being taken out of their own country illegally.

ARTICLE 12 You have the right to say what you think should happen when adults are making decisions that affect you, and to have your opinions taken into account.

ARTICLE 13 You have the right to get, and to share, information as long as the information is not damaging to yourself or others.

ARTICLE 14 You have the right to think and believe what you want and to practise your religion, as long as you are not stopping other people from enjoying their rights. Parents should guide children on these matters.

ARTICLE 15 You have the right to meet with other children and young people and to join groups and organisations, as long as this does not stop other people from enjoying their rights.

ARTICLE 16 You have the right to privacy. The law should protect you from attacks against your way of life, your good name, your family and your home.

ARTICLE 17 You have the right to reliable information from the mass media. Television, radio and newspapers should provide information that you can understand, and should not promote materials that could harm you.

ARTICLE 18 Both parents share responsibility for bringing up their children, and should always consider what is best for each child. Governments should help parents by providing services to support them, especially if both parents work.

ARTICLE 19 Governments should ensure that children are properly cared for, and protect them from violence, abuse and neglect by their parents or anyone else who looks after them.

ARTICLE 20 If you cannot be looked after by your own family, you must be looked after properly, by people who respect your religion, culture and language.

ARTICLE 21 If you are adopted, the first concern must be what is best for you. The same rules should apply

Children's rights

whether the adoption takes place in the country where you were born or if you move to another country.

ARTICLE 22 If you are a child who has come into a country as a refugee, you should have the same rights as children born in that country.

ARTICLE 23 If you have a disability, you should receive special care and support so that you can live a full and independent life.

ARTICLE 24 You have the right to good quality health care and to clean water, nutritious food and a clean environment so that you can stay healthy. Rich countries should help poorer countries achieve this.

ARTICLE 25 If you are looked after by your local authority rather than your parents, you should have your situation reviewed regularly.

ARTICLE 26 The government should provide extra money for the children of families in need.

ARTICLE 27 You have a right to a standard of living that is good enough to meet your physical and mental needs. The government should help families who cannot afford to provide this.

ARTICLE 28 You have a right to an education. Discipline in schools should respect children's human dignity. Primary education should be free. Wealthy countries should help poorer countries achieve this.

ARTICLE 29 Education should develop your personality and talents to the full. It should encourage you to respect your parents, your own and other cultures and the environment.

ARTICLE 30 You have a right to learn and use the language and customs of your family whether or not these are shared by the majority of the people in the country where you live.

ARTICLE 31 You have a right to relax, play and join in a wide range of activities.

ARTICLE 32 The government should protect you from work that is dangerous or might harm your health or education.

ARTICLE 33 The government should provide ways of protecting you from dangerous drugs.

ARTICLE 34 The government should protect you from sexual abuse.

ARTICLE 35 The government should ensure that you are not abducted or sold.

ARTICLE 36 You should be protected from any activities that could harm your development.

ARTICLE 37 If you break the law, you should not be treated cruelly. You should not be put in a prison with adults and you should be able to keep in contact with your family.

ARTICLE 38 Governments should not allow children under 16 to join the army. In war zones, you should receive special protection.

ARTICLE 39 If you have been neglected or abused, you should receive special help to restore your self-respect.

ARTICLE 40 If you are accused of breaking the law, you should receive legal help. Prison sentences for children should only be used for the most serious offences.

ARTICLE 41 If the laws of a particular country protect you better than the articles of the Convention, then those laws should stay.

ARTICLE 42 The government should make the Convention known to all parents and children.

Articles 43-54 are about how adults and governments should work together to make sure all children get all their rights.

Your call

All people have rights, but also the responsibility to make sure their behaviour doesn't stop others getting their rights.

www.unicef.org.uk

Child labour

GLOBALLY, ONE IN SIX CHILDREN WORK. Around 60% of these children work in hazardous conditions, such as in mines or in agriculture using dangerous machinery, chemicals or pesticides. An estimated 8.4 million children are trapped in the worst forms of child labour including slavery, trafficking, debt bondage, prostitution, work in armed conflict, pornography and other illicit activities.

What is child labour?

Not all children's work is child labour. Child labour is work that is exploitative or likely to be hazardous; work that interferes with child's education or is harmful to their health or physical and emotional development. In its worst forms, child labour involves children being separated from their families, living in slavery-like conditions or being exposed to serious hazards and illnesses.

Safe, light, part-time, legal work that does not affect children's health and personal development or interfere with their schooling is not child labour and is generally regarded as a positive experience.

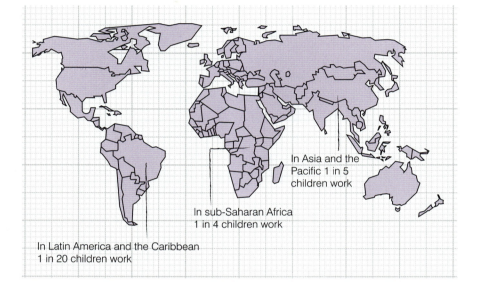

In Asia and the Pacific 1 in 5 children work

In sub-Saharan Africa 1 in 4 children work

In Latin America and the Caribbean 1 in 20 children work

Mini glossary

hazardous – *dangerous*

pesticides – *chemicals used to kill pests such as insects*

illicit – *illegal*

livelihoods – *jobs or sources of income*

www.savethechildren.org.uk

The information on these pages is reprinted with kind permission from Save the Children.
© Save the Children

Facts and figures

▶ **218 million** children aged 5-17 are involved in child labour worldwide.

▶ **126 million** children work in hazardous conditions.

▶ **22,000** working children die each year in work-related accidents.

▶ **8.4 million** children are involved in the worst forms of child labour.

▶ **300,000** children are involved in armed conflict.

▶ **1.2 million** children are trafficked each year into exploitative work in mines, factories, armed conflict or sex work.

▶ The highest numbers of child labourers are in the Asia/Pacific region where there are **122 million** working children.

▶ The highest proportion of child labourers is in Sub Saharan Africa, where **26%** of children (49 million) are involved in work.

▶ **69%** of child labourers work in the agricultural sector.

▶ **22%** of child labour is in the services sector, including working for traders, in restaurants and hotels and domestic work.

▶ **9%** of child labour is in industry, mining and construction.

Child labour

Why do children work?

Poverty

Poverty is one of the major factors pushing children into work. In situations of extreme poverty, families depend upon children's income for survival. Children who suffer most from discrimination are more likely to be forced into the worst jobs.

Access to good-quality education

Children can be pushed into work because they lack access to good-quality education. Their families may be unable to afford the costs of schooling or the poor quality of education on offer means that they decide that work offers them better opportunities for developing skills.

Culture

Culture and tradition affect attitudes to work. In some communities, work is seen to be the best option for teaching children the skills they will need as adults.

Vulnerable situations

Conflict, natural disaster, severe illness or economic change can increase the risk of children becoming entangled in child labour. The death of family members, disruption to livelihoods and the risk of separation of children from their families place children at increased risk of exploitation. In regions badly affected by HIV/AIDS, for example, children may have to work to support the household when adults become sick or die.

Nasrin's Story

Nasrin is 15 years old and attends the Prodipan Working Children's Education Centre in Dhaka, which Save the Children supports. Nasrin works seven days a week to earn money that she gives to her mother to buy food for the family and to pay rent. She is one of six children. Her father hasn't worked since he broke his leg.

❝ I have been working at the shoe brush factory for about three or four years. I beat the bristles, tie them together with a pin and press them into the wooden handle. It's hard work. I scratch my hands on the wooden handle… The factory environment is not so good – it's very dirty and smelly. I feel very bad working there. If the environment were clean then I wouldn't feel so sick to work there. Even if I don't like working in the factory, what can I do about it? I have to earn money. ❞

Why is child labour harmful?

Work can deny children their rights to protection and education and lead to irreversible health problems, psychological damage and even death. Children are exposed to abuse, long working hours and poor working conditions without any way to seek help. They may be forced to carry heavy loads, use harmful substances or dangerous machinery without protection. They do not have time for play or education that is vital to a child's development.

The invisible nature of some types of work, such as domestic work, places children at increased risk of sexual and other types of abuse. Research by Save the Children in India, for example, shows that the average working day of most child domestic workers is 15 hours long and that 68% of the child participants interviewed in the research have faced physical abuse and 86% emotional abuse.

ST. MARY'S UNIVERSITY COLLEGE
A COLLEGE OF THE QUEEN'S UNIVERSITY OF BELFAST

Your rights

Do all children get their right to life?

Poverty is the main cause for the deaths of millions of children every year. The Millennium Development Goals aim to cut the number of children who die before their fifth birthday, but the world isn't doing enough to make sure this happens.

Do all children get their right to health?

Around the world, 270 million children don't have access to basic health care. 800 million children don't get enough food to eat and 40 per cent of the world's people don't have access to safe water and sanitation. Meanwhile, hundreds of millions of children worldwide aren't getting the protection they need to keep them safe and healthy.

Do all children get their right to protection?

Hundreds of millions of children are missing out on the protection they need. Millions suffer from abuse and neglect. 180 million children do dangerous work. It's thought that 1.2 million children are trafficked every year, while over a million children are in jails around the world. It's thought that 30,000 child soldiers are now being used in conflicts.

Do all children get their right to education?

Around the world, 121 million children are still missing out on their education. Girls are more likely than boys to miss out on school, while the hardest-to-reach children need extra help to get them into education.

Do all children get their rights?

Do all children get their right to identity?

Every year, millions of children are excluded and invisible. One of the reasons for this is that their births are not registered – so governments and other agencies don't know that they exist. In the UK, campaigners argue that Anti-Social Behaviour Orders and the 'naming and shaming' of children denies them their right to privacy.

Do all children get their right to opinions?

Some children get the chance to participate in decisions that affect them and some organisations, such as the UN, are getting better at listening to children's views. But too many children still feel that their opinions are ignored. Young people are having their say about the media, and some are even making their own news reports.

Do all children get their right to play?

Children miss out on their right to play for many reasons. Conflicts, and the landmines they leave behind, can make play too dangerous. Child labour means many children don't have time to play, while many children who are orphaned by AIDS miss out on their childhoods because their forced to work and look after their brothers and sisters.

Mini glossary

Millennium Development Goals – *eight goals that world leaders agreed to achieve by 2015 in order to tackle extreme poverty*

sanitation – *services to improve hygiene and protect health, such as clean water and disposal of waste*

www.unicef.org.uk

All equal?

WE'VE ALL GROWN UP believing children are different. In a sense, they are: they're younger than everyone else – but they're still people, they've still got feelings, and, like adults, they still need some respect. Yet children aren't taken seriously; until they're 18, nothing they say or do really makes any difference.

I've spent the past 15 years of my life being a kid, so I know what it's like to be one. When I walk home from school, I see signs outside the shops, over and over again: 'two children at a time'; 'no bags'; even little printed notices barring you completely 'unless accompanied by an adult'. Imagine if you were a child: waiting forever for your turn, and even then, watching the adults push you away, stroll into the shop, neither knowing nor caring how long you've been there. And why? Because they're adults.

I often go out to watch a film at the local cinema, as many of my friends do. The thing is, once you're over 15, you pay the same amount as an adult. Even though you can't work (at least without a special permit), you have to pay just as much as those who have a job. And you don't qualify for the minimum wage. It gets worse when you realise that the price of cinema tickets drops again if you're an adult and in full-time education like we are. We earn little or nothing, but we pay more.

A few years ago the local council decided to change the catchment areas for our local schools, each of which offers different opportunities, and is therefore better suited to different people. The council launched a consultation, yet they sought the opinions of our parents, not us.

Perhaps, this year, things may start to change. CRAE recently released an extensive report on how well the Government is protecting children's rights. A delegation of 12 children from around England then presented the report to a UN Committee in Geneva, Switzerland, who will then take the issues further.

www.getreadyforchange.org.uk

So what does this report – written and researched by children – actually say about children, and whether they're given the respect they deserve? In fact, quite a lot. They raised the issue of whether children are treated fairly in the media: the sweeping generalisations and unsupported stereotypes they are faced with. They identified particular groups which respected children least, such as councillors and MPs, bus drivers, and shop assistants.

They found huge numbers of children were discriminated against racially, and that very few knew how to formally complain if adults seriously abused them. They found that only around half of children had been consulted following a divorce as to which parent they would live with.

Unsurprisingly, they raised the issue of whether older children – those above 16 – should be allowed to vote. These children can leave home, marry, apply for a job, fight and even die for their country, and yet still not vote; they can also, crucially, pay taxes to a government they don't even have a right to vote for.

CRAE's message to the UN is crucial for so many children, many of whom are subjected to abuses far more serious than children in my area will ever be faced with. The UN takes children seriously; the government, so far, hasn't. Politicians never grow tired of that age-old sentiment: 'children are our future'. What they fail to realise, or perhaps simply overlook, is that children are our present too. Perhaps, just for once, they'll listen.

By Adam Roberts, age 15. 4 July 2008

Smacking

What do we want?

We simply want children to have equal protection. 'Smacking' is already banned for all people except children. The law still allows parents and others to justify common assault of children as 'reasonable punishment'. This defence is unjust and unsafe, and must be abolished now. This simple reform will send a clear message that hitting children, however we dress it up, is as unacceptable and unlawful as hitting anyone else. Children are people with human rights to physical integrity and human dignity just like the rest of us.

> **DID YOU KNOW?**
>
> *In 2004, the MORI Social Affairs Institute found that seven in ten British people (71 per cent) support a change in the law to give children equal protection from being hit in the family home.*

www.childrenareunbeatable.org.uk

The information on this page is reprinted with kind permission from the Children are Unbeatable! Alliance. © Children are Unbeatable! Alliance

Ten reasons to support equal protection

❶ Human rights obligations

The United Nations Committee on the Rights of the Child has twice recommended law reform; the European Social Charter requires abolition of all corporal punishment, and the European Court of Human Rights has ruled that UK law does not provide enough protection.

❷ Children are being legally hit

Research commissioned by the Department of Health shows that most UK children are hit and around a third are hit severely (Smith and Nobes, 1997).

❸ Support child protection professionals

All those involved in protecting children from abuse, from the NSPCC to Social Services Directors, want the law changed to provide a clear basis for child protection.

❹ Promote positive parenting

The law as it stands undermines the work of health visitors, midwives, early years carers and many others who try to promote positive, non-violent discipline.

❺ Cultural change

The law sets standards in every area of society, including family relationships. How can we expect parents to stop hitting their children if the law says it's acceptable?

❻ Reform works

Children are given equal protection from assault in Germany, Sweden, Denmark, Austria and many other countries, changing attitudes and behaviour for the better.

❼ The law is outdated

The law allowing children to be legally hit dates back to the 19th century and is out of step with the values of a modern society.

❽ People do not oppose change

Most people support changing the law to give children equal protection (MORI Social Affairs Institute, 2004).

❾ It's the right thing to do

Many countries have changed their laws without having public opinion firmly on their side. They did it because it is the right thing to do for children, children's rights and child protection, and public attitudes have changed as a result.

❿ Hitting children is wrong

...and the law should say so.

Smacking is a decision for parents

The age-old question of whether parents should smack their children.

A Parliamentary amendment seeking to ban smacking outright was never even put to MPs during the recent debate on the Children and Young Person's Bill. This, I have to say, came as some relief: the smacking debate is both well-worn and tricky. The clause, however, was supported by 100 Labour MPs, and its failure was lamented by Tony Samphier of the Children Are Unbeatable! Alliance, who rather dramatically said that ministers should now be conscience-stricken over the 'hurt that every child feels while being legally assaulted'.

For once, however, I find myself in agreement with Beverley Hughes, the Children's Minister, who recently wrote that 'we do not encourage or condone smacking… neither do we support a ban which would make smacking a crime' That, she said, would mean that criminal charges could be brought against a mother who gave her child a mild smack on the hand for refusing to put back sweets grabbed at the supermarket check-out.

The trouble with opposing, however mildly, something like the Children Are Unbeatable! Alliance is that it makes one sound like some bewhiskered lunatic who staunchly believes that children should be beatable. The anti-smacking campaigners always talk about 'hitting' and 'assaulting' children, rather than smacking, but a sharp tap on the hand of a child who is about to run across a busy road, for example, would not be my definition of assault.

I understand the arguments. I am not a smacker myself, partly because the difference in size between me and my two-and-a-half year old son would make such an action feel vaguely grotesque. Nor do I believe that – in the midst of a tantrum, say – it would do more than urge him to greater heights of confused rage. But I know loving parents who smack their children lightly as a means of disciplining them in extreme circumstances, and the idea of them being hauled off for police questioning on the say-so of some eagle-eyed stranger is deeply disturbing in itself.

We are not talking here about parents who hit their children with serious force, or to the point of leaving a mark or a weal. That is quite a different matter, and to pretend that it is part and parcel of the same thing is to go against common sense.

There is, perhaps, no issue that so clearly marks the difference in attitudes between the older and younger generations as that of physical punishment. Many adults from the generations that grew up before and immediately after the Second World War were deeply conflicted on the matter: they saw it almost as a duty by which they must shape the willful nature of the child, and yet they felt ashamed at their own ugly loss of control in enacting it.

My late grandfather was caned, aged eight, by a young female teacher for falling asleep at his school desk: he was woken by the searing pain of the blow. Such brutal practices have rightly been outlawed, but the orthodoxy has swung to the opposite extreme. Authority figures such as teachers and policemen are now effectively forbidden from making any decisive physical response to unruly teenagers.

Hulking boys of 14 and 15, who suffer no such inhibitions when it comes to shoving around their younger or weaker schoolmates, chant the Childline number if a teacher lays a restraining hand on them. A policeman who picked a cheeky teenager up and briefly placed him in a bin in 2005, to the loud laughter of the boy's friend, was given a written warning and the boy received £4,000 in compensation.

Out of control adolescents have got the message that not only are they unbeatable, they are also untouchable. The consequences for the rest of society are frequently unthinkable.

By Jenny McCartney, 12 October 2008

Mini glossary

amendment – addition or change to a document

lamented – mourned for

condone – excuse or overlook; approve of

assault – violent attack

orthodoxy – commonly accepted opinion

compensation – payment given to make up for injury or suffering

Activities

Brainstorm

Brainstorm to find out what you know about children's rights.

1. What is the United Nations Convention on the Rights of the Child?

    ....

    ....

2. What is child labour? Why is it harmful?

    ....

    ....

    ....

Oral activities

3. In a group, brainstorm all the rights you think every young person around the world should have. Are there any rights you think that adults should have but children should not? Why is this?

    NOTES...

    ....

    ....

4. Sometimes it's hard for young people to make themselves heard. With a partner, give a short speech explaining why you think children's rights in particular need to be protected, in the UK and around the world.

    NOTES...

    ....

Moral Dilemmas

5. You are out shopping and have found an item of clothing you really want to buy. However, there have been reports that the company which makes the product uses child labour in its factories. Do you buy the item anyway?

6. 'Smacking children should be a decision for parents.' Do you agree with this statement? Do you think parents should be allowed to discipline their children by smacking them, or does smacking violate children's rights?

Activities

Research activities

7. Do some research into children's rights in a developing country. What laws are in place to protect children in the country you have researched? How well are children's rights there protected when compared to a developed country like the UK?

   NOTES..

   ....

   ....

   ....

   ....

8. Visit the Children's Rights Alliance for England website at www.getreadyforchange.org.uk. How successfully do you think the site addresses the issues that are important to young people?

   NOTES..

   ....

   ....

   ....

Written activities

Complete the following activities in your exercise books or on a sheet of paper.

9. Read the article *All equal?* on page 23. Write an article exploring any ways in which you have felt your own rights have been ignored in the past.

10. Read the article *Child labour* on pages 20-21. Write a diary entry for a young person the same age as you who has to work in hazardous conditions to support their family and doesn't have the chance to go to school. How would their life differ from the lives of you and your friends?

Design activities

11. Many young people are not aware of their rights. Create a leaflet for young people outlining their rights, using the article *Children's rights* on pages 18-19 as a starting point. Explain the rights which are protected by the United Nations Convention on the Rights of the Child in your own words, selecting those which you feel to be most important and illustrating them with cartoons.

Key Facts

▶ *Human rights belong to everyone. They are the basic rights we all have simply because we are human, regardless of who we are, where we live or what we do. (page 1)*

▶ *No one can have their human rights completely taken away – even if they have not met their responsibilities or have compromised the rights of others. (page 2)*

▶ *The modern concept of human rights has its foundations in the Universal Declaration of Human Rights, adopted by the United Nations in the aftermath of the Second World War. However, the ideas behind human rights have been present throughout history in many different societies and civilizations. (page 6)*

▶ *It is estimated that there are some 27 million slaves across the globe today. (page 10)*

▶ *The largest number of slaves in the world live in Pakistan, India and Nepal, where as many as 18 million workers are held as slaves – working for generations to repay small loans. (page 11)*

▶ *60% of men and 50% of women surveyed agreed with the statement 'Britain should have, and use, the right to deport foreigners suspected by the intelligence services, even if there is not enough courtroom evidence to bring them to trial, and they might be sent to countries where they could be tortured'. (page 13)*

▶ *The Human Rights Act is a written law passed in 1998 which is in force in England and Wales. The human rights that are contained within this law are based on the articles of the European Convention on Human Rights. (page 14)*

▶ *Every child and young person under 18 has rights and responsibilities. They're protected by the United Nations Convention on the Rights of the Child. It's been signed by every country in the world, except the USA and Somalia. (page 18)*

▶ *Globally, one in six children work. Around 60% of these children work in hazardous conditions, such as in mines or in agriculture using dangerous machinery, chemicals or pesticides. An estimated 8.4 million children are trapped in the worst forms of child labour including slavery, trafficking, debt bondage, prostitution, work in armed conflict, pornography and other illicit activities.* **(page 20)**

▶ *Around the world, 121 million children are still missing out on their education. (page 22)*

▶ *Research commissioned by the Department of Health shows that most UK children are hit and around a third are hit severely. (page 24)*

Glossary

Child labour – *Child labour is work that is exploitative or likely to be hazardous; work that interferes with a child's education, or work that is harmful to their health or physical and emotional development.*

Corporal punishment – *Punishing somebody by inflicting pain on them.*

Discrimination – *Treating a person or group of people differently or unfairly because of their race, colour, nationality, ethnic or national origin.*

European Convention on Human Rights – *The Convention was adopted by the Council of Europe in 1950 to enshrine the articles of the Universal Declaration of Human Rights in laws. The UK signed up to the Convention in 1951.*

Exploitation – *When somebody uses another person or treats them unfairly for selfish reasons.*

Human rights – *The basic rights all human beings are entitled to, regardless of who they are, where they live or what they do. Concepts of human rights have been present throughout history, but our modern understanding of the term emerged as a response to the horrific events of the Holocaust.*

The Human Rights Act – *The Human Rights Act is a written law (statute) passed in 1998 which is in force in England and Wales. The human rights that are contained within this law are based on the articles of the European Convention on Human Rights.*

Prostitution – *Engaging in sexual activity with another person in exchange for money.*

Slavery – *A slave is someone who is denied their freedom, forced to work without pay and considered to be literally someone else's property. Although slavery is officially banned internationally, there are an estimated 27 million slaves worldwide.*

Torture – *Deliberately causing a person physical or mental pain or suffering in order to get information from them or force them to make a confession.*

Trafficking – *The transport and/or trade of people from one area to another, usually for the purpose of forcing them into labour or prostitution. According to 2005 statistics from the International Labour Organisation, 2.45 million people are victims of trafficking annually, of which 50% are children.*

United Nations Convention on the Rights of the Child (UNCRC) – *An international human rights treaty that protects the rights of all children and young people under 18. The UK signed the convention on 19 April 1990, ratified it on 16 December 1991 and it came into force in the UK on 15 January 1992. When a country ratifies the convention it agrees to do everything it can to implement it. Every country in the world has signed the convention except the USA and Somalia.*

Universal Declaration of Human Rights – *The first international agreement on what were formerly called 'the rights of man', which came about from the desire of the world's governments to prevent the recurrence of the horrific events of the Second World War by setting out a shared bill of rights for all peoples and all nations. The text is non-binding, but it is the main authority on human rights, and has been supported by the UN's ongoing work to encourage its incorporation into domestic laws.*